# Unmasking and Defeating Social Media Scammers

# Chapter Titles:

The Digital Frontier
The Lurking Threat
Unveiling the Mask
The Art of Deception
Beware the Phisher men.
The Trojan Horse Tactic
The Rise of the Bots
The Dark Side of Influence
Cyber Extortion Chronicles
Protecting Your Digital Fort
The Power of Digital Literacy
Cybersecurity for All
The Resilient Online Community
Fighting Back: Real Stories
A Scammer-Free Future

# Book Introduction:

In an age where the digital world intertwines seamlessly with our daily lives, the internet has become a breeding ground for a new kind of menace - social media scammers. These insidious individuals, hidden behind screens and false identities, are constantly scheming to exploit the unsuspecting users of major social media channels. Welcome to "Guardians of the Virtual Realm: Unmasking and Defeating Social Media Scammers."

The internet is a double-edged sword. On one side, it connects us, empowers us, and opens doors to a world of knowledge and possibilities. On the other, it harbors threats that can jeopardize our privacy, financial security, and emotional well-being. For the uninitiated, navigating this digital wilderness can be akin to stumbling into a dark alley in the middle of the night.

This book is your flashlight in that alley, your guide through the labyrinth of social media scams. We will delve deep into the tactics employed by scammers, exploring their dark arts and revealing their true intentions. We'll unmask the wolves in sheep's clothing and teach you how to recognize the subtle signs of deception. But this book is not just about awareness; it's about empowerment.

Within these pages, you'll find not only tales of individuals who fell victim to these virtual predators but also stories of resilience and redemption. You'll discover the tools and strategies to protect yourself, your loved ones, and your digital community. Knowledge is your armor, and this book will equip you to be a guardian of the virtual realm.

It's time to take back control, to fortify your defenses, and to create a safer online world for yourself and those around you. Let's embark on this journey together, where we shine a light on the darkness of social media scams and emerge as guardians of the virtual realm.

# Chapter 1: The Digital Frontier

In the early days of the internet, it was a place of wonder and exploration. A vast frontier where pioneers could connect, share, and create. But just as the Wild West had its outlaws, this digital frontier has its own brand of troublemakers - social media scammers.

The internet has come a long way since its inception. It has evolved from a simple network of interconnected computers to a global phenomenon that touches almost every aspect of our lives. With this evolution came the rise of social media, platforms that allow us to share our lives, connect with friends and family, and even conduct business. However, with the benefits of these platforms came an unintended consequence - the rise of social media scammers.

Social media scammers are individuals or groups who use these platforms to deceive, manipulate, and exploit unsuspecting users. They are the modern-day con artists, and the internet is their playground. They lurk in the shadows of your favorite social media channels, waiting for the perfect opportunity to strike.

Imagine this: You receive a friend request from an attractive stranger. They claim to have similar interests and a shared connection. You accept the request, and before you know it, you're engaged in a conversation that seems friendly enough. But behind the friendly facade lies a hidden agenda - to steal your personal information, your money, or even your identity.

This is just one of the many tactics employed by social media scammers. They are masters of disguise, experts at crafting convincing personas, and adept at exploiting human psychology. In this chapter, we will explore the origins of social media scams, their evolution, and the reasons behind their proliferation in the digital age.

But fear not, for knowledge is your first line of defense. By understanding the digital frontier and the threats it harbors, you can begin to arm yourself against the lurking dangers. Join us on this journey as we unveil the true nature of social media scammers and learn how to protect yourself in this brave new world.

# Chapter 2: The Lurking Threat

In the vast expanse of the internet, social media scammers are the predators silently stalking their prey. They blend in seamlessly with the online community, waiting for the opportune moment to strike. This chapter will delve deeper into the lurking threat posed by these digital manipulators and help you recognize their presence.

## The Chameleon Effect

One of the most unsettling aspects of social media scammers is their ability to morph into whatever you desire. They study your online presence, identify your interests, and craft a persona that seems tailor-made for you. If you're a fan of outdoor adventures, they become avid hikers. If you're passionate about photography, suddenly they're an aspiring photographer too. This chameleon-like adaptability makes them incredibly convincing.

## The Bait and Hook

Scammers often dangle an irresistible lure to reel you in. It could be an alluring promise of easy money, an attractive romance, or a golden opportunity that seems too good to be true. They exploit basic human desires and vulnerabilities. In their hands, curiosity becomes a trap, and hope turns into a snare.

## The Emotional Manipulation

Social media scammers are not just after your money or personal information; they're also after your emotions. They know that by forging a connection and building trust, they can manipulate your feelings. They'll shower you with compliments, listen to your problems, and pretend to be your confidant. They become the shoulder to cry on, all while plotting their next move.

## The Power of Anonymity

The digital world offers a cloak of anonymity that emboldens scammers. They hide behind screen names and stolen photos, making it difficult to track them down. This anonymity grants them a sense of invincibility, enabling them to take risks they wouldn't dare in the real world.

## The Financial Consequences

While some scams are emotionally distressing, others can have severe financial repercussions. Scammers may trick you into investing in bogus ventures, buying nonexistent products, or giving away your bank details. The consequences can be devastating, leaving victims in financial ruin.

## The Psychological Toll

The aftermath of falling victim to a social media scam is often marked by shame, guilt, and anger. Victims blame themselves for being deceived, and the emotional scars can run deep. It's crucial to understand that anyone can be targeted, and there is no shame in seeking help or reporting the incident.

## Your Shield: Awareness

To defend yourself against the lurking threat of social media scammers, awareness is your strongest shield. By understanding their tactics and recognizing the signs, you can thwart their attempts. Remember, scammers rely on deception, and when you shine a light on their actions, their power diminishes.

In the upcoming chapters, we will unveil the techniques scammers use, their tricks of the trade, and the psychological strategies they employ. By equipping yourself with this knowledge, you'll be better prepared to navigate the digital landscape and protect yourself from the lurking threat of social media scammers. Stay vigilant, for the virtual realm holds both wonder and peril, and it's up to you to safeguard your digital sanctuary.

# Chapter 3: Unveiling the Mask

In our ongoing quest to understand and combat social media scammers, we now turn our attention to a crucial aspect: unveiling the mask they hide behind. Just as a magician's trick loses its allure once you know the secret, scammers lose their power when their true identities are revealed.

# The Art of Deception

Social media scammers are skilled in the art of deception. They create personas that appear genuine, often using stolen photos and fabricated stories. To unveil their mask, you must become a digital detective, scrutinizing the details that don't add up. Here are some red flags to watch for:

- **Inconsistencies**: Scammers may slip up and provide conflicting information. Pay close attention to their stories and check for any discrepancies.
- **Fake Photos**: Use reverse image searches to check if the photos they've shared belong to someone else. Scammers often steal images from the internet.
- **Grammar and Language**: Many scammers operate from countries

where English is not the first language. Poor grammar and unusual language use can be a sign.

- **Too Good to Be True**: If their stories or offers seem too perfect, they probably are. Scammers promise the world to ensnare their victims.

# The Anatomy of a Scammer's Profile

To better identify a scammer, let's dissect the common elements of their online profiles:

1. **Stolen Photos**: As mentioned earlier, scammers often use stolen images. You can use reverse image searches on platforms like Google to check if these images appear elsewhere on the internet.
2. **Limited Connections**: Scammers typically have a small number of connections or friends. This is because maintaining fake profiles

can be challenging with a large network.

3. **Impersonal Content**: Their posts and interactions tend to be generic and impersonal. They may avoid sharing personal details about themselves.

4. **Too Much Flattery**: Scammers often shower you with compliments and affection early on. Be wary of overly enthusiastic admirers.

5. **Requests for Money**: Scammers often create elaborate stories to elicit sympathy and money from their victims. These stories can range from medical emergencies to financial crises.

# Real-Life Detectives: The Scammer Sleuths

There are online communities of individuals who have made it their mission to unmask scammers. They collaborate to identify and expose fraudulent profiles, helping protect others from falling victim. You can also report suspicious accounts to the social media platform in question, which can act against them.

# Your Digital Toolkit

To unveil the mask of social media scammers, arm yourself with the following tools and techniques:

- **Reverse Image Search**: Use tools like Google Reverse Image Search to check the authenticity of photos shared by the individual.
- **Verify Information**: Cross-check the information they provide, such as job titles, locations, or personal histories.
- **Trust Your Instincts**: If something feels off or too good to be true, trust your gut. It's better to be cautious than regretful.
- **Report Suspected Scammers**: Most social media platforms have mechanisms to report suspicious accounts. Use them to protect yourself and others.

By learning to spot the inconsistencies and red flags, you become a digital detective capable of unveiling the mask of social media scammers. In the next chapter, we will delve even deeper into the techniques these scammers employ, including the notorious "phishing" tactics. Stay vigilant, for knowledge is your greatest weapon against those who seek to deceive you in the virtual realm.

# Chapter 4: The Art of Deception

Social media scammers are modern-day illusionists, masters of the digital sleight of hand. In this chapter, we will explore the intricate techniques they use in their art of deception. Understanding these tactics will empower you to see through the smoke and mirrors and protect yourself against their tricks.

## The Phishing Expedition

One of the most prevalent scams in the digital realm is phishing. Phishing attacks involve scammers posing as trustworthy entities to trick you into revealing sensitive information, such as login credentials or credit card details. Here's how they do it:

- **Email Spoofing**: Scammers send emails that appear to come from legitimate sources, like banks or social media platforms. These emails often contain urgent messages, enticing you to click on links that lead to fake login pages.

- **Fake Websites**: Scammers create convincing replica websites that mimic those of reputable companies. These sites are designed to capture your login information, and you may not realize you're on a fake page.
- **Impersonation**: Some scammers impersonate trusted individuals, such as tech support agents or friends, to gain your trust. They then manipulate you into divulging sensitive data.

# The Impersonation Game

Scammers are adept at impersonating real people or institutions. They may:

- **Impersonate Friends**: By hacking into the accounts of your friends, they gain access to your personal network and exploit the trust you have in your connections.

- **Fake Profiles**: Scammers create profiles that closely resemble those of celebrities, influencers, or authority figures. They then use these profiles to lure unsuspecting victims.

# Emotional Manipulation

Scammers know that emotions can cloud judgment. They exploit this by playing on your feelings of fear, greed, or curiosity. For instance:

- **Fear Tactics**: They may send you alarming messages, claiming your account is compromised or that you owe money, to prompt a hasty reaction.
- **Fake Romance**: Romance scammers create fake personas and forge emotional connections with their victims, eventually requesting money or personal information.

# Social Engineering

Social engineering is psychological manipulation technique scammers use to gain your trust and manipulate you into revealing information or taking certain actions. Techniques include:

- **Pretexting**: Scammers create a fabricated scenario, like pretending to be a co-worker in trouble, to elicit information or assistance from you.
- **Baiting**: They tempt you with something desirable, such as a free download, to entice you into taking actions that compromise your security.

# The Overarching Goal: Information

Whether it's through phishing, impersonation, emotional manipulation, or social engineering, the ultimate objective of scammers is to obtain information. This information can be used for identity theft, fraud, or further manipulation.

# Your Shield: Vigilance

To protect yourself from the artful deception of social media scammers, stay vigilant:

1. **Verify Email Sources**: Always check the sender's email address in suspicious emails. Legitimate institutions use official domains.
2. **Beware of Urgency**: Scammers often create a sense of urgency. Pause, verify, and don't rush into decisions.
3. **Double-Check URLs**: Before entering sensitive information on a website, ensure it's the legitimate site by inspecting the URL and looking for "https://" and a padlock symbol.
4. **Guard Personal Information**: Avoid sharing personal or financial details online, especially with strangers.

5. **Educate Yourself**: Stay informed about the latest scam tactics, so you can recognize them.

By understanding the art of deception employed by social media scammers, you can become a savvy digital detective. In the next chapters, we'll explore the rise of automated threats like bots and the dark side of social influence. Remember, knowledge is your greatest ally in the virtual realm, where deception can be as elusive as it is dangerous.

# Chapter 5: Beware the Phisher men.

As we journey deeper into the realm of social media scams, one breed of scammers stands out—the Phisher men. These clever deceivers use bait to lure unsuspecting victims into their webs. In this chapter, we'll cast our net into the tactics and techniques of these digital anglers and teach you how to avoid getting caught.

## The Bait and the Hook

Phisher men are aptly named; they cast a wide net of deception and wait for curious or unsuspecting victims to take the bait. Their bait often takes the form of:

- **Fake Emails**: Phisher men send emails that look remarkably genuine, often impersonating trusted organizations such as banks, e-commerce sites, or social media platforms. These emails might contain alarming messages, enticing you to click on links.
- **Spoofed Websites**: The links in these emails often lead to well-crafted replica websites that closely resemble the legitimate ones. Victims are then prompted to enter sensitive information like login credentials or credit card details.

## Signs of Phishing

To avoid falling prey to Phisher men, look for these telltale signs:

- **Generic Greetings**: Phishing emails often start with generic greetings like "Dear User" instead of using your name.
- **Urgency**: They create a sense of urgency, pressuring you to act quickly. Be wary of emails that claim your account will be suspended unless you take immediate action.
- **Misspelled URLs**: Check the URL in the address bar of any website you visit. Phisher men often use slightly altered URLs that are easy to overlook.
- **Poor Grammar and Spelling**: Phishing emails often contain errors in grammar and spelling. Legitimate organizations typically proofread their communications.
- **Check the Sender's Email Address**: Examine the sender's email address closely. Phisher men often use email addresses that mimic official ones but have subtle differences.

# Protecting Yourself from Phishing

Defending against phishing requires a combination of caution and awareness:

1. **Verify the Source**: If you receive an email requesting sensitive information or urging immediate action, independently verify its authenticity by contacting the organization through official channels.
2. **Use Security Software**: Install reputable antivirus and anti-phishing software to provide an additional layer of protection against phishing attempts.
3. **Educate Yourself**: Familiarize yourself with the common tactics used in phishing attacks and share this knowledge with friends and family.

4. **Enable Two-Factor Authentication**: Whenever possible, enable two-factor authentication on your accounts. This adds an extra layer of security even if your credentials are compromised.
5. **Hover Over Links**: Hover your cursor over links in emails to preview the actual URL before clicking on them.

# Reporting Phishing

If you receive a phishing email or come across a phishing website, it's crucial to report it. Most email providers and social media platforms have mechanisms for reporting suspicious content. By reporting phishing attempts, you can help protect not only yourself but also others who may be targeted.

In our next chapter, we will uncover another facet of the social media scam landscape—the Trojan Horse tactic. Understanding this insidious strategy will further fortify your defenses against online deception. Remember, when it comes to phishing, staying informed and vigilant is your best defense against getting hooked by the Phisher men's bait.

# Chapter 6: The Trojan Horse Tactic

In the world of social media scams, the Trojan Horse tactic is a sinister stratagem employed by scammers to infiltrate your digital defenses. Named after the legendary ruse used to infiltrate Troy, this tactic involves disguising harmful intent within an innocent-looking facade. In this chapter, we will unveil the workings of the digital Trojan Horse and show you how to spot and defend against it.

## The Deceptive Disguise

The Trojan Horse is all about disguise. In the famous tale of Troy, the Greeks constructed a massive wooden horse to appear as a gift, concealing soldiers within. Similarly, online scammers use attractive bait to hide malicious intent. This can take various forms:

- **Fake Software**: Scammers might offer seemingly useful software, promising enhanced functionality or security tools. Once installed, these programs could compromise your device.

- **Infected Attachments**: Emails or messages might contain attachments that appear legitimate but harbor malware or viruses. Opening them can lead to your system's compromise.
- **Free Downloads**: Be cautious of offers for free downloads or files shared by unknown sources. They could contain harmful payloads.

## The Trojan Horse's Path

Once you unwittingly invite a digital Trojan Horse into your realm, it can cause various forms of damage:

1. **Malware Delivery**: Trojans can deliver malware to your device, which may steal your data, monitor your activities, or allow unauthorized access.

2. **Keylogging**: Some Trojans record your keystrokes, including login credentials and financial information, which are then sent to the attacker.
3. **Backdoor Access**: Trojans can create a secret backdoor into your device, allowing attackers to control it remotely without your knowledge.
4. **System Corruption**: In some cases, Trojans can corrupt or damage your files and operating system, rendering your device unusable.

# Recognizing the Trojan Horse

To safeguard yourself against the Trojan Horse tactic, you must learn to recognize its signs:

- **Unsolicited Downloads**: Be cautious of downloading software or files from unknown or unverified sources.

- **Unusual Behavior**: If your device starts behaving strangely—slowing down, crashing, or displaying unusual pop-ups—it could be a sign of a Trojan infection.
- **Unexpected Emails or Messages**: Be wary of emails or messages from unknown senders, especially if they contain attachments or links.

# Defending Against the Trojan Horse

Defending against the Trojan Horse tactic requires a combination of caution and digital hygiene:

1. **Trustworthy Sources**: Only download software or files from reputable sources. Avoid pirated software and unofficial download sites.
2. **Security Software**: Install and regularly update reputable antivirus and anti-malware software to detect and remove Trojans.

3. **Email Scrutiny**: Be cautious of email attachments, especially if they come from unknown sources. Don't open attachments unless you're sure of their legitimacy.
4. **Keep Software Updated**: Regularly update your operating system and software to patch vulnerabilities that Trojans may exploit.
5. **Use a Firewall**: Enable a firewall on your device to block unauthorized access.

# Reporting Suspicious Activity

If you suspect your device has been compromised or if you come across a potentially harmful download or attachment, report it to your IT department or a cybersecurity professional. Timely action can help mitigate the damage.

Understanding the Trojan Horse tactic is another step toward becoming a vigilant guardian of your digital realm. In the next chapter, we will explore the rise of automated threats in the form of bots, which have become formidable players in the world of social media scams. Remember, knowledge is your shield against the Trojan Horses that may attempt to breach your digital defenses.

# Chapter 7: The Rise of the Bots

In the intricate ecosystem of social media, the rise of the bots marks a significant turning point. Bots are automated scripts designed to mimic human behavior online, and they play a pivotal role in the realm of social media scams. In this chapter, we'll uncover the mechanics of these digital actors and how to distinguish them from genuine interactions.

# The Bot Invasion

Bots come in various shapes and sizes, and they can serve both benign and malevolent purposes. While some bots are used for legitimate tasks like automating customer support, others are deployed for deceitful ends. Here's how they operate:

- **Social Media Bots**: These bots are programmed to engage with users on platforms like Twitter, Facebook, and Instagram. They can follow accounts, like posts, share content, and even engage in conversations.
- **Spambots**: Spambots flood social media with unsolicited messages, advertisements, and links. They can clutter your feed and compromise your online experience.

- **Impersonation Bots**: Some bots impersonate real users or influencers, attempting to gain followers and trust. They often promote products, services, or scams.

## Signs of Bot Activity

Detecting bot activity can be challenging because they are designed to mimic human behavior. However, there are telltale signs that can help you identify them:

1. **Uniformity**: Bots tend to have a pattern of activity. They may retweet the same posts, use similar language, or follow a specific set of accounts in quick succession.
2. **Limited Content**: Bots often lack original content. They primarily share or repost existing material without adding value.
3. **Excessive Activity**: Bots can be incredibly active, posting or

interacting around the clock with no downtime.

4. **Inorganic Growth**: Accounts that suddenly gain thousands of followers in a short time may be using bots to boost their numbers.

5. **Lack of Personal Information**: Bots typically have scant personal information in their profiles and may use generic profile pictures.

# The Dark Side of Bots

Bots are not inherently malicious, but they can be harnessed for harmful purposes:

- **Spreading Misinformation**: Bots can be used to amplify fake news, disinformation, and propaganda, influencing public opinion and sowing discord.
- **Scam Promotion**: Some bots promote fraudulent schemes or products, luring unsuspecting users into financial scams.

- **Identity Theft**: Bots can impersonate real individuals, potentially causing reputational harm and confusion.

# Defending Against Bots

To protect yourself from bot manipulation on social media:

1. **Vet Your Followers**: Regularly review your followers and unfollow or block suspicious accounts.
2. **Check Account Activity**: Be cautious of accounts that exhibit signs of bot activity, such as excessive posting or repetitive content.
3. **Use Bot Detection Tools**: Some online tools and browser extensions can help identify bot accounts.
4. **Stay Informed**: Be aware of current events and trends to spot bot-driven misinformation.

5. **Report Suspected Bots**: Report suspicious accounts to the respective social media platform.

# Reporting Bot Activity

Reporting bot activity is essential to maintaining the integrity of social media platforms. By flagging suspicious accounts, you contribute to a safer online environment for all users.

As we delve deeper into the world of social media scams, the next chapter will explore the influence wielded by scammers over their victims through persuasive tactics. Understanding the dark side of influence will empower you to recognize and resist their manipulative strategies. Remember, knowledge is your armor against the automated threats that lurk in the virtual realm.

# Chapter 8: The Dark Side of Influence

In the intricate dance of social media scams, influence plays a pivotal role. Scammers, like puppeteers, pull the strings of their victims, manipulating emotions, trust, and desires. In this chapter, we'll shine a light on the dark side of influence, revealing the psychological tactics scammers use to control their targets.

## The Power of Persuasion

Persuasion is the art of convincing someone to do something, and it's a tool that scammers wield with expertise. They tap into fundamental human psychology, exploiting vulnerabilities and desires. Here are some of the key persuasive tactics they use:

1. **Appealing to Emotions**: Scammers often evoke strong emotions like fear, excitement, or sympathy. Emotional responses can cloud judgment and lead to impulsive decisions.
2. **Social Proof**: They create an illusion of popularity or trustworthiness by showcasing fake testimonials, endorsements, or many supposed followers.
3. **Authority**: Scammers may pose as experts, using official-sounding titles or affiliations to gain credibility and trust.
4. **Urgency**: They play on your fear of missing out (FOMO) by creating a sense of urgency. Limited time offers or threats of consequences if you don't act quickly can be compelling.
5. **Reciprocity**: Scammers often offer something of perceived value for free, creating a sense of

indebtedness. Victims may feel compelled to reciprocate by complying with their requests.

6. **Scarcity**: By presenting opportunities as rare or exclusive, scammers make them seem more desirable. This can lead to impulsive decisions to seize the perceived limited chance.

# Persuasion in Action

Let's examine how these tactics are applied in real-life scenarios:

- **Romance Scams**: Scammers pose as potential romantic partners, showering victims with affection and emotional support. They create a deep emotional connection, making victims more likely to comply with their requests, which often involve sending money.

- **Investment Scams**: Scammers promise incredible returns on investments, often playing on victims' desire for financial security and wealth. They use urgency and authority to push victims into making quick decisions.
- **Tech Support Scams**: Impersonating tech support agents, scammers prey on the fear of computer viruses or hacking. They create a sense of urgency and authority, convincing victims to pay for unnecessary services or share personal information.

# Resisting Manipulation

Recognizing the dark side of influence is the first step to resisting manipulation by scammers:

1. **Critical Thinking**: Question information and offers that seem too good to be true. Take your time to evaluate and research before making decisions.

2. **Emotional Awareness**: Be mindful of your emotional responses when interacting online. If something triggers a strong emotional reaction, step back and analyze the situation.
3. **Fact-Checking**: Verify information independently, especially before sharing or acting on social media.
4. **Consult Trusted Sources**: Seek advice from trusted friends, family, or professionals when making important decisions.
5. **Privacy Settings**: Review and strengthen your privacy settings on social media to limit exposure to potential scammers.

# Reporting Manipulative Tactics

If you encounter persuasive tactics used by scammers, report the accounts or content to the respective social media platforms. Timely reporting helps protect others from falling victim to the same manipulation.

In our next chapter, we will delve into the harrowing stories of individuals who have been ensnared by social media scams. By understanding the real-life consequences of online deception, we can further fortify ourselves against the dangers that lurk in the virtual world. Remember, knowledge is your shield against the puppeteers who seek to control your digital strings.

# Chapter 9: Cyber Extortion Chronicles

In the shadows of the digital realm, a nefarious breed of scammers specializes in a chilling art form—cyber extortion. These individuals use various techniques to coerce and manipulate their victims, leaving them feeling vulnerable and trapped. In this chapter, we'll explore the harrowing tales of those who have fallen victim to cyber extortion and highlight the strategies to protect yourself.

# The Anatomy of Cyber Extortion

Cyber extortionists exploit fear, embarrassment, and the desire to protect one's reputation or personal information. They often employ the following tactics:

1. **Revenge Porn**: Scammers threaten to release explicit photos or videos unless their victims comply with demands.
2. **Ransomware Attacks**: Extortionists encrypt a victim's data and demand a ransom for its release.

3. **Financial Blackmail**: Victims are coerced into sending money under the threat of personal or financial information being exposed.
4. **Online Shaming**: Extortionists threaten to publicize sensitive or embarrassing information unless their victims meet their demands.

# Victims' Ordeals

1. **Sarah's Tale of Revenge Porn**: Sarah, a young professional, shared intimate photos with a partner she trusted. When their relationship soured, her partner threatened to release those photos to her family and employer unless she paid a hefty sum. Fearing the repercussions, Sarah complied, but the emotional scars remained.
2. **Mark's Ransomware Nightmare**: Mark, a small business owner, fell victim to a ransomware attack that locked him out of his company's critical data. The extortionists demanded a substantial ransom in

cryptocurrency, threatening to permanently delete the data if he refused. Mark had no choice but to pay, dealing a crippling blow to his business.

3. **Lisa's Brush with Financial Blackmail**: Lisa received an email from an anonymous sender who claimed to have obtained her financial records. The extortionist threatened to expose her financial situation to her colleagues and friends unless she wired a significant amount of money. Overcome with fear and embarrassment, Lisa complied, but her trust in online interactions was shattered.

# Protecting Yourself from Extortion

Cyber extortion is a chilling reality, but there are steps you can take to protect yourself:

1. **Be Wary of Sharing Intimate Content**: Think twice before sharing intimate photos or videos, even with trusted partners. Once shared, you lose control over their distribution.
2. **Regularly Back Up Data**: Regularly back up your data to secure locations to mitigate the impact of ransomware attacks.
3. **Use Strong Passwords**: Strengthen your online security with strong, unique passwords for different accounts.
4. **Enable Two-Factor Authentication (2FA)**: Whenever possible, activate 2FA on your accounts for an added layer of security.
5. **Stay Informed**: Educate yourself about the tactics cyber extortionists use and remain vigilant.
6. **Seek Legal Help**: If you become a victim of cyber extortion, consult legal authorities and cybersecurity professionals for guidance.

# Reporting Cyber Extortion

If you encounter cyber extortion or receive threats, report them to the relevant authorities immediately. Timely reporting can help prevent further victimization.

In the upcoming chapters, we will delve into strategies for protecting yourself and your loved ones from falling prey to social media scams. By understanding the stories and consequences of these harrowing experiences, we aim to arm you with the knowledge and resilience needed to navigate the digital landscape safely. Remember, knowledge is your greatest defense against the dark arts of cyber extortion.

# Chapter 10: Protecting Your Digital Fortress

As we navigate the treacherous waters of social media scams and cyber extortion, it's vital to establish a robust defense to protect your digital fortress. In this chapter, we will explore practical strategies to fortify your online presence and keep both yourself and your loved ones safe from harm.

## The Sentinel's Toolkit

Imagine yourself as the vigilant sentinel guarding your digital castle. These tools and techniques will help you stand strong against the threat of social media scams:

1. **Privacy Settings**: Regularly review and update the privacy settings on your social media profiles. Restrict access to personal information and posts to trusted connections only.
2. **Verify Requests**: Before accepting friend or connection requests, verify the authenticity of the profiles. Scammers often use fake accounts to gain access to your network.
3. **Educate Yourself**: Stay informed about the latest scam tactics and phishing methods. Knowledge is your first line of defense.
4. **Use Strong Passwords**: Create strong, unique passwords for your accounts, and consider using a reputable password manager to keep them secure.
5. **Enable Two-Factor Authentication (2FA)**: Activate 2FA on your accounts whenever possible. This provides an extra layer of security by requiring a

code sent to your mobile device or email for login.

6. **Beware of Unsolicited Messages**: Be cautious of unsolicited messages, especially those containing links or attachments. Verify the sender's identity before clicking on anything.

7. **Verify Suspicious Requests**: If someone asks for personal information, money, or assistance, independently verify their identity. Scammers often create convincing sob stories to manipulate their victims.

# Strengthening Family and Friends

Your protection extends to your family and friends. Share these strategies with them to create a united front against social media scams:

1. **Communication**: Encourage open communication about online interactions and potential scams.

Create a safe space for sharing concerns.
2. **Teach Vigilance**: Educate your loved ones about the signs of scams, such as unsolicited friend requests, odd messages, or suspicious links.
3. **Practice Safe Sharing**: Advise them to be cautious about sharing personal information online and to set strict privacy settings.
4. **Password Hygiene**: Encourage the use of strong, unique passwords and the activation of 2FA.
5. **Verify Before Trusting**: Teach them the importance of verifying the authenticity of online contacts before trusting them with personal or financial information.

## Reporting Scams

If you encounter or suspect a social media scam, promptly report it to the relevant authorities or the platform in question. Reporting not only protects you but also helps prevent others from becoming victims.

## Seeking Professional Help

In cases of cyber extortion or severe online harassment, it may be necessary to seek the assistance of legal and cybersecurity professionals. They can guide you through the process of mitigating the damage and pursuing legal action if needed.

By arming yourself with knowledge and adopting these protective measures, you become a formidable sentinel guarding your digital fortress. In the subsequent chapters, we will uncover the strategies scammers use to infiltrate your trust and gain access to your personal information. Remember, in the digital realm, your vigilance and proactive measures are your most potent weapons against the lurking threat of social media scams.

# Chapter 11: The Trust Trap

Trust is the cornerstone of social interactions, both in the real world and the digital realm. However, scammers exploit this fundamental human trait to deceive and manipulate. In this chapter, we will delve into the strategies scammers use to gain your trust and access your personal information, and we'll equip you with the tools to spot and resist the trust trap.

# The Art of Gaining Trust

Scammers are skilled at building rapport and trust with their potential victims. They employ several tactics to establish a sense of credibility and authenticity:

1. **Impersonation**: They often impersonate trustworthy entities such as banks, government agencies, or well-known companies. These impersonations can be convincing, with official logos and email addresses.
2. **Fake Profiles**: Scammers create fake social media profiles that seem genuine. They use stolen photos, invent life stories, and mimic the interests of their targets.
3. **Familiar Language**: Scammers use language that resonates with their targets, making them feel like

they're communicating with someone who shares their values and interests.

4. **Testimonials**: Some scammers feature fake testimonials or reviews from supposed satisfied customers to bolster their credibility.
5. **References**: They may claim to have mutual friends or acquaintances to further establish trust.

## The Trust Trap in Action

Let's examine how these tactics play out in real-life scenarios:

- **Phishing Emails**: Scammers send emails that appear to be from a trusted source, like a bank or a government agency. The email may contain urgent messages, enticing you to click on a link and enter sensitive information on a fake website.
- **Romance Scams**: Scammers build romantic relationships with

their targets, often over a long period. They may create elaborate backstories and use emotional manipulation to gain trust and eventually ask for money.

- **Tech Support Scams**: Impersonating tech support agents, scammers claim there's a problem with your device or account. They offer to help, gaining access to your system and potentially stealing personal information.

# Trust Trap Detection

To avoid falling into the trust trap, develop a keen sense of skepticism:

1. **Verify the Source**: Always independently verify the identity of individuals or organizations contacting you, especially if they're requesting sensitive information.
2. **Check Email Addresses**: Scrutinize email addresses carefully. Legitimate organizations typically use official domains.

3. **Examine Profiles**: When interacting with individuals on social media, review their profiles for inconsistencies and suspicious activity. Use reverse image searches to check if their photos appear elsewhere on the internet.

4. **Be Cautious of Unsolicited Offers**: If you receive unsolicited offers that seem too good to be true, approach them with skepticism. Trust your instincts.

# Reporting Suspicious Activity

If you encounter the trust trap or suspicious interactions, report them to the relevant authorities or the social media platform. Your actions could prevent others from falling victim to the same deception.

In the upcoming chapters, we will explore the psychological techniques scammers use to manipulate emotions and persuade their targets to comply with their demands. By understanding these tactics, you'll be better equipped to resist their influence and protect your digital security. Remember, trust is an asset, but in the digital realm, it's essential to verify before you trust.

# Chapter 12: The Influence Game

In the world of social media scams, scammers are skilled manipulators who play a dangerous influence game. They use psychological techniques to sway emotions, shape decisions, and compel their targets to comply with their demands. In this chapter, we'll unveil the psychological tactics employed by scammers and equip you with the knowledge to resist their influence.

## The Persuasive Arsenal

Scammers draw from a persuasive arsenal that taps into human psychology. Some of the key techniques they employ include:

1. **Fear Tactics**: Scammers exploit fear by creating a sense of urgency or impending doom. They may claim your account is compromised or that dire consequences will follow if you don't act immediately.

2. **Emotional Manipulation**: They understand that emotions can cloud judgment. Scammers may use sympathy, empathy, or even flattery to manipulate emotions and build rapport with their victims.
3. **Social Proof**: Scammers often showcase fake testimonials, endorsements, or a large number of supposed followers to create an illusion of popularity or trustworthiness.
4. **Authority**: Some scammers pose as experts, using official-sounding titles or affiliations to gain credibility and trust.
5. **Reciprocity**: By offering something of perceived value for free, scammers create a sense of indebtedness. Victims may feel compelled to reciprocate by complying with their requests.
6. **Urgency**: Scammers create a fear of missing out (FOMO) by presenting opportunities as limited time offers or by threatening

negative consequences if you don't act quickly.

# The Influence Game in Action

Let's explore how these tactics manifest in real-life scenarios:

- **Romance Scams**: Scammers build emotional connections with their targets, exploiting their desire for love and companionship. They manipulate emotions, create trust, and eventually request money or personal information.
- **Investment Scams**: Scammers promise lucrative returns on investments, playing on the victim's desire for financial security and wealth. Urgency and authority are often used to push victims into making hasty decisions.
- **Tech Support Scams**: Impersonating tech support agents, scammers prey on the fear of computer viruses or hacking. They create a sense of urgency and

authority, convincing victims to pay for unnecessary services or share personal information.

# Resisting the Influence

To protect yourself from falling victim to the influence game, cultivate a vigilant mindset:

1. **Critical Thinking**: Question information and offers that seem too good to be true. Take your time to evaluate and research before making decisions.
2. **Emotional Awareness**: Be mindful of your emotional responses when interacting online. If something triggers a strong emotional reaction, step back and analyze the situation.
3. **Fact-Checking**: Verify information independently, especially before sharing or taking action on social media.
4. **Consult Trusted Sources**: Seek advice from trusted friends, family,

or professionals when making important decisions.

5. **Privacy Settings**: Review and strengthen your privacy settings on social media to limit exposure to potential scammers.

# Reporting Manipulative Tactics

If you come across manipulative tactics or suspect that you're being targeted, report the accounts or content to the respective social media platform. Timely reporting helps protect not only yourself but also others who may be vulnerable to manipulation.

In our next chapter, we will delve into the world of online scams and reveal the strategies scammers use to defraud individuals and organizations. By understanding these scams, you'll be better prepared to recognize and avoid them. Remember, in the influence game, knowledge is your armor against manipulation.

# Chapter 13: Unmasking Online Scams

In the vast expanse of the internet, online scams are like hidden traps waiting to ensnare unsuspecting victims. Scammers employ various strategies to defraud individuals and organizations, leaving financial and emotional turmoil in their wake. In this chapter, we'll shine a light on the most common online scams and provide you with the knowledge to recognize and steer clear of them.

## The Landscape of Online Scams

Online scams come in many shapes and sizes, but they share common characteristics:

1. **Deceptive Appearances**: Scammers often create the illusion of legitimacy by using professional-looking websites, official logos, or familiar branding.
2. **Urgency**: They create a sense of urgency, pressuring victims to act quickly to prevent losses or seize an opportunity.
3. **Lack of Transparency**: Scammers often conceal key details about their operations, making it difficult for victims to make informed decisions.
4. **Promises of Easy Money**: Many scams promise quick and substantial financial gains with minimal effort, preying on individuals' desires for wealth.
5. **Social Engineering**: Scammers use social engineering techniques to manipulate victims emotionally and psychologically, making them

more likely to comply with their demands.

# Common Online Scams

Let's explore some of the most prevalent online scams:

1. **Phishing Scams**: Scammers impersonate trusted entities through emails or websites, luring victims into revealing sensitive information such as login credentials, credit card numbers, or social security numbers.
2. **Advance Fee Fraud**: Victims are promised a large sum of money, a job, or a valuable item in exchange for a fee or personal information. Once the fee is paid, the promised reward never materializes.
3. **Online Auction and Shopping Scams**: Scammers post fake products for sale online, often at attractive prices. Victims pay for the products but never receive them.

4. **Tech Support Scams**: Victims receive unsolicited calls or messages claiming their computer has a virus or security issue. Scammers request payment for unnecessary services or gain remote access to steal information.
5. **Romance Scams**: Scammers build romantic relationships online, often over an extended period. They eventually request money or personal information from their victims.

# Recognizing Online Scams

To avoid falling victim to online scams, develop a vigilant eye for these telltale signs:

1. **Too Good to Be True**: Be skeptical of offers that promise substantial financial gains or opportunities with little effort.
2. **Urgency and Pressure**: Scammers often use time-sensitive

language to create urgency. Take your time to research and verify.

3. **Unsolicited Communication**: Be cautious of unsolicited emails, calls, or messages, especially those requesting personal or financial information.
4. **Lack of Transparency**: If a website or individual is not forthcoming with essential information, proceed with caution.
5. **Verify Sources**: Independently verify the legitimacy of organizations or individuals before engaging in financial transactions or sharing personal information.

# Reporting Online Scams

If you encounter an online scam or suspect fraudulent activity, report it to relevant authorities, such as your local law enforcement agency or the appropriate online platform. Reporting helps protect others from falling victim to the same scam.

In the next chapter, we will explore the world of cyberattacks and cybersecurity, shedding light on the tactics employed by malicious actors to compromise digital security. By understanding these threats, you'll be better prepared to defend yourself and your digital assets. Remember, in the online landscape, knowledge is your shield against scams and fraud.

# Chapter 14: Guardians of Cybersecurity

In the ever-evolving digital landscape, the concept of cybersecurity has become paramount. Cyberattacks, both large and small, threaten individuals, organizations, and nations alike. In this chapter, we will delve into the tactics employed by malicious actors to compromise digital security and explore strategies to safeguard your digital assets.

# The Threat Landscape

Cyberattacks take various forms, each with its own set of objectives and techniques:

1. **Malware**: Malicious software, including viruses, Trojans, and ransomware, is designed to infiltrate and compromise computer systems.
2. **Phishing**: Attackers use deceptive emails or messages to trick recipients into revealing sensitive information or clicking on malicious links.
3. **Social Engineering**: Malicious actors manipulate individuals into

divulging confidential information or performing actions that compromise security.

4. **Distributed Denial of Service (DDoS)**: Attackers overwhelm a target system with a flood of traffic, rendering it inaccessible to users.

5. **Data Breaches**: Sensitive data, such as login credentials or financial information, is stolen from organizations or individuals.

6. **Cyber Espionage**: State-sponsored or criminal groups infiltrate computer systems to gather intelligence, steal intellectual property, or disrupt operations.

# Strengthening Cybersecurity

Protecting your digital assets requires proactive measures and awareness:

1. **Antivirus Software**: Install reputable antivirus and anti-malware software to detect and remove threats.

2. **Regular Updates**: Keep your operating system, software, and applications up to date to patch vulnerabilities.
3. **Strong Passwords**: Create strong, unique passwords for each account and use a password manager to securely store them.
4. **Two-Factor Authentication (2FA)**: Enable 2FA whenever possible to add an extra layer of security.
5. **Email Scrutiny**: Be cautious of unsolicited emails, especially those with attachments or links. Verify the sender's authenticity.
6. **Data Encryption**: Use encryption tools to protect sensitive data during transmission and storage.
7. **Employee Training**: Educate yourself and employees about cybersecurity best practices and how to recognize threats.

# The Role of Cybersecurity Professionals

In the face of increasing cyber threats, cybersecurity professionals play a crucial role:

1. **Threat Detection**: They employ advanced tools and techniques to identify and analyze potential threats.
2. **Incident Response**: Cybersecurity teams are prepared to respond swiftly and effectively to mitigate the impact of cyberattacks.
3. **Security Education**: They provide ongoing training and awareness programs to empower individuals and organizations to protect themselves.
4. **Policy Development**: Cybersecurity professionals create and implement security policies and practices to safeguard digital assets.

# Reporting Cyber Incidents

If you encounter or suspect a cyber incident, report it to your organization's

IT department or a cybersecurity professional. Timely reporting can help contain the threat and prevent further damage.

As we approach the final chapter of this book, we will explore the steps you can take to recover and rebuild in the aftermath of a cyberattack or online scam. Understanding the path to recovery is vital in an age where digital resilience is paramount. Remember, in the world of cybersecurity, knowledge is your greatest defense.

# Chapter 15: Rise from the Ashes: Recovery and Resilience

In the wake of a cyberattack or falling victim to an online scam, the path to recovery can be challenging, both emotionally and practically. In this final chapter, we'll explore the steps you can take to rebuild and emerge stronger from such experiences. Resilience in the face of adversity is the goal.

## The Aftermath

Whether it's a cyberattack that compromises your digital security or an online scam that leaves you financially drained, the aftermath can be overwhelming. Emotions like fear, anger, and shame may flood your thoughts. Here's how to navigate this challenging period:

1. **Emotional Support**: Reach out to friends, family, or a therapist for emotional support. Talking about your experience can help you process your feelings.
2. **Report the Incident**: If you've been a victim of a cyberattack or scam, report it to the relevant authorities and organizations. This step is crucial in preventing further harm.
3. **Legal Recourse**: Depending on the nature of the incident, consider seeking legal advice or assistance. Cyberattacks often have legal consequences, and pursuing justice can be part of your recovery.

# Rebuilding Digital Security

After a cyber incident, it's vital to rebuild your digital security:

1. **Change Passwords**: Change passwords for compromised accounts and use strong, unique ones. Consider enabling 2FA where possible.
2. **Scan for Malware**: Run a thorough antivirus scan on your devices to ensure no malware remains.
3. **Secure Your Accounts**: Review and strengthen your privacy settings on social media and online accounts.
4. **Update Software**: Ensure all your software, including your operating system and applications, is up to date to patch vulnerabilities.
5. **Data Backup**: Regularly back up your data to secure locations to mitigate data loss in future incidents.

# Learning and Growing

Turn adversity into an opportunity for growth:

1. **Education**: Learn from your experience. Educate yourself about common scams and cyber threats to become a more vigilant digital citizen.
2. **Digital Resilience**: Develop digital resilience. Understand that cyber incidents can happen to anyone, and that recovery is possible.
3. **Support Others**: Share your experience with others to raise awareness and support those who may be going through similar challenges.
4. **Advocate for Change**: Advocate for stronger cybersecurity measures in your workplace or community to protect others.

# Conclusion: Your Digital Journey Continues

The digital landscape is ever-changing, and the threats that lurk within it continue to evolve. By arming yourself with knowledge, vigilance, and a resilient spirit, you can navigate this landscape with confidence.

This book has taken you on a journey through the dark alleys of social media scams, cyber extortion, influence tactics, online scams, and cybersecurity. It's our hope that you now possess the tools and understanding to protect yourself and your loved ones in the digital realm.

Your digital journey continues, and with each step, you become more resilient and better equipped to face the challenges of the online world. Remember, in the face of adversity, you have the power to rise from the ashes and emerge stronger than ever.

# Appendix: Additional Resources

To further assist you in your digital journey, we've compiled a list of additional resources that provide valuable information, guidance, and support in the realm of online safety and cybersecurity:

1. **Federal Trade Commission (FTC)**: The FTC offers resources on a wide range of topics, including identity theft, online scams, and consumer protection. Visit their website for practical advice and updates on the latest scams.
   Website: https://www.ftc.gov/
2. **Stay Safe Online**: This website provides tips, resources, and best practices for staying safe in the digital world. It covers topics like online privacy, cybersecurity, and safe online shopping.
   Website: https://staysafeonline.org/
3. **Cybersecurity & Infrastructure Security Agency (CISA)**: CISA offers insights into current cybersecurity threats and provides guidance on securing your online presence. Their resources cater to individuals, businesses, and government agencies.

Website: https://www.cisa.gov/

4. **National Cyber Security Centre (NCSC)**: The NCSC, part of the UK government, provides advice and guidance on cybersecurity for individuals and organizations. Their resources cover topics like password security and phishing awareness.

Website: https://www.ncsc.gov.uk/

5. **Online Safety Research**: Stay informed about the latest research and publications on online safety and cybersecurity. Organizations like the Pew Research Center and the Cybersecurity and Infrastructure Security Agency (CISA) regularly publish reports on relevant topics.

   - Pew Research Center: https://www.pewresearch.org/
   - CISA Publications: https://www.cisa.gov/publications-library

6. **Local Cybersecurity Resources**: Check with your local government

or law enforcement agencies for cybersecurity resources and advice specific to your region. Many local agencies offer guidance on reporting cyber incidents.

7. **Cybersecurity Forums and Communities**: Join online communities and forums dedicated to cybersecurity discussions. These platforms provide a space for sharing experiences and seeking advice from experts and peers.

Remember that the digital landscape is constantly evolving, and staying informed is a crucial aspect of your digital safety. By utilizing these resources and continuing to educate yourself, you'll be better prepared to navigate the digital world with confidence and resilience. Your journey toward digital safety and security is ongoing, and with the right tools and knowledge, you can face any challenge that comes your way.

# Acknowledgments

Writing a comprehensive book on the topics of social media scams, cyber extortion, online influence, scams, cybersecurity, and recovery is a collaborative effort that involves the contributions and support of many individuals and organizations.

We would like to extend our gratitude to the following:

- The cybersecurity experts, researchers, and professionals who tirelessly work to enhance digital safety and security for individuals, organizations, and society.
- The countless victims of online scams and cyberattacks who have bravely shared their stories and experiences, shedding light on the real-world consequences of these threats.
- The organizations and government agencies that provide valuable

resources and support to combat cyber threats and promote online safety.

- The individuals and organizations who tirelessly educate and advocate for digital safety and cybersecurity awareness.
- Our readers, whose commitment to learning and staying safe online drives the need for resources like this book.

Remember, in the digital age, knowledge is your most potent defense. Stay safe, stay informed, and stay vigilant. Your digital journey continues, and with the right knowledge and resources, you can navigate it with confidence and resilience.

# *End of Book*

Thank you for embarking on this journey through the digital landscape with us. In an era where the online world plays an increasingly central role in our lives, understanding the risks and equipping ourselves with knowledge is paramount.

We hope this book has provided you with valuable insights, practical strategies, and a heightened awareness of the threats that lurk in the digital realm. Remember, you have the power to protect yourself and your loved ones from social media scams, cyber extortion, online influence tactics, scams, and cybersecurity threats.

Your digital journey is ongoing, and as you continue to explore the vast and ever-changing landscape of the internet, carry with you the lessons learned here. Stay safe, stay informed, and stay vigilant. Your digital resilience is your greatest asset.

With warm regards, Anthony (Author)

www.ingramcontent.com/pod-product-compliance
Lightning Source LLC
LaVergne TN
LVHW051717050326
832903LV00032B/4256